Sobriety
COLORING
BOOK JOURNAL

Date _____ M ☐ T ☐ W ☐ T ☐ F ☐ S ☐ S ☐

One goal for today

_____

Today's positive affirmation

_____

_____

My mood today   Did I stay sober today?

★ ★ ★ ★ ★   YES ☐   NO ☐

Was today's goal accomplished?

YES ☐   NO ☐

What I am grateful for today

_____

_____

_____

What I am proud of today

_____

_____

My plans for tomorrow

_____

Additional thoughts

Today's sketch

Date _____ M ☐ T ☐ W ☐ T ☐ F ☐ S ☐ S ☐

One goal for today

_____

Today's positive affirmation

_____

_____

My mood today   Did I stay sober today?

⭐ ⭐ ⭐ ⭐ ⭐   YES ☐   NO ☐

Was today's goal accomplished?

YES ☐   NO ☐

What I am grateful for today

_____

_____

_____

What I am proud of today

_____

_____

My plans for tomorrow

_____

_____

Additional thoughts

Today's sketch

Date _____ M ☐ T ☐ W ☐ T ☐ F ☐ S ☐ S ☐

One goal for today

_____

Today's positive affirmation

_____

My mood today   Did I stay sober today?

★ ★ ★ ★ ★   YES ☐   NO ☐

Was today's goal accomplished?

YES ☐   NO ☐

What I am grateful for today

_____

_____

_____

What I am proud of today

_____

_____

My plans for tomorrow

_____

_____

Additional thoughts

Today's sketch

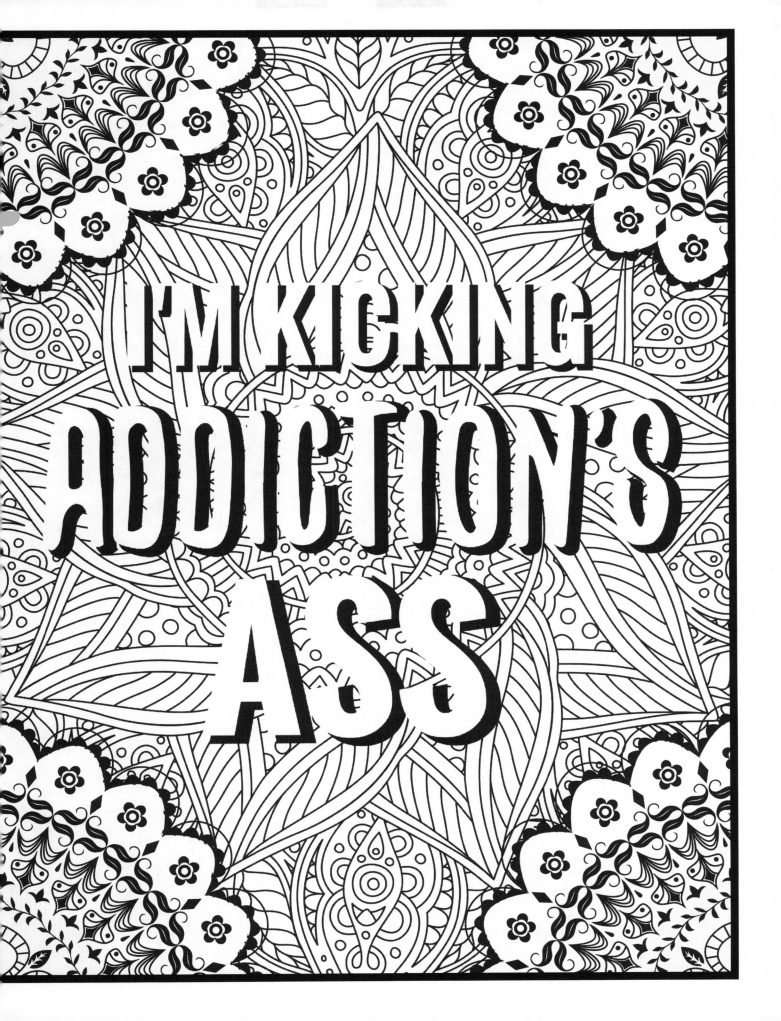

Date _____ M ☐ T ☐ W ☐ T ☐ F ☐ S ☐ S ☐

One goal for today

_____

Today's positive affirmation

_____

_____

My mood today	Did I stay sober today?

⭐ ⭐ ⭐ ⭐ ⭐   YES ☐   NO ☐

Was today's goal accomplished?

YES ☐   NO ☐

What I am grateful for today

_____

_____

_____

What I am proud of today

_____

_____

My plans for tomorrow

_____

_____

Additional thoughts

Today's sketch

Date _____ M ☐ T ☐ W ☐ T ☐ F ☐ S ☐ S ☐

One goal for today

_____

Today's positive affirmation

_____

My mood today   Did I stay sober today?

★ ★ ★ ★ ★   YES ☐   NO ☐

Was today's goal accomplished?

YES ☐   NO ☐

What I am grateful for today

_____

_____

What I am proud of today

_____

_____

My plans for tomorrow

_____

Additional thoughts

_____

_____

_____

_____

_____

_____

_____

_____

Today's sketch

Date _____ M ☐ T ☐ W ☐ T ☐ F ☐ S ☐ S ☐

One goal for today

_____

Today's positive affirmation

_____

_____

My mood today   Did I stay sober today?

⭐ ⭐ ⭐ ⭐ ⭐   YES ☐   NO ☐

Was today's goal accomplished?

YES ☐   NO ☐

What I am grateful for today

_____

_____

_____

What I am proud of today

_____

_____

_____

My plans for tomorrow

_____

_____

Additional thoughts

Today's sketch

Date _____ M ☐ T ☐ W ☐ T ☐ F ☐ S ☐ S ☐

One goal for today

_____

Today's positive affirmation

_____

_____

My mood today   Did I stay sober today?

★ ★ ★ ★ ★   YES ☐   NO ☐

Was today's goal accomplished?

YES ☐   NO ☐

What I am grateful for today

_____

_____

_____

What I am proud of today

_____

_____

_____

My plans for tomorrow

_____

_____

Additional thoughts

Today's sketch

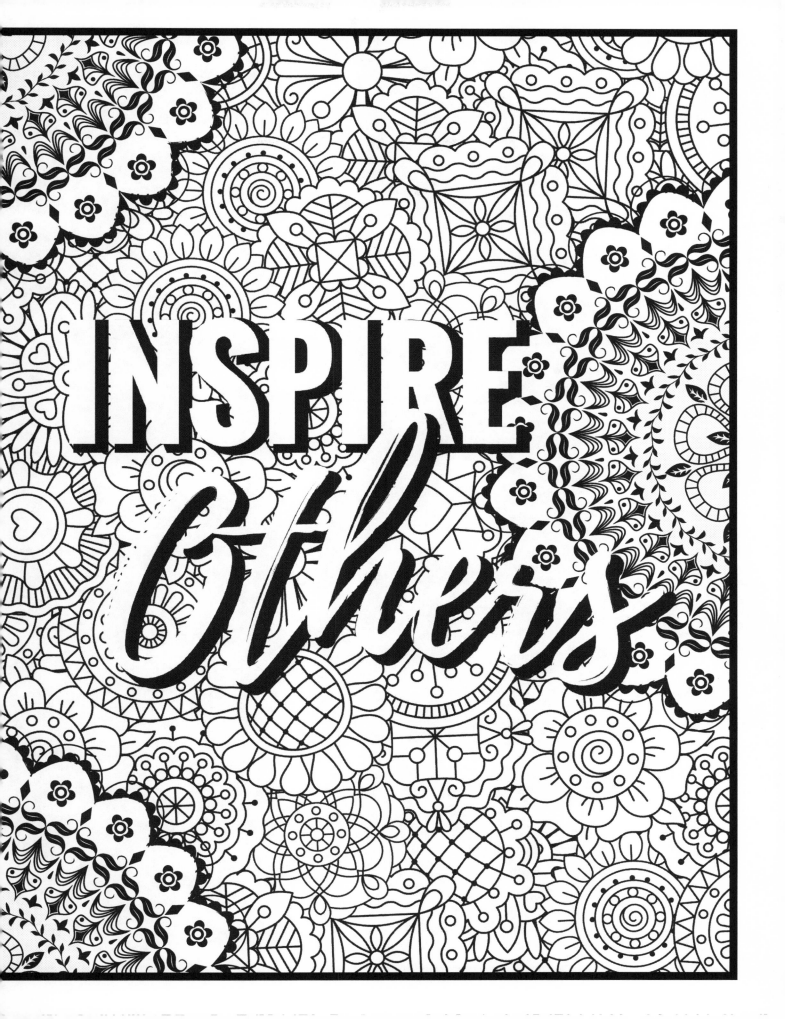

Date _____ M ☐ T ☐ W ☐ T ☐ F ☐ S ☐ S ☐

One goal for today

_____

Today's positive affirmation

_____

_____

My mood today   Did I stay sober today?

★ ★ ★ ★ ★   YES ☐   NO ☐

Was today's goal accomplished?

YES ☐   NO ☐

What I am grateful for today

_____

_____

_____

What I am proud of today

_____

_____

My plans for tomorrow

_____

_____

Additional thoughts

Today's sketch

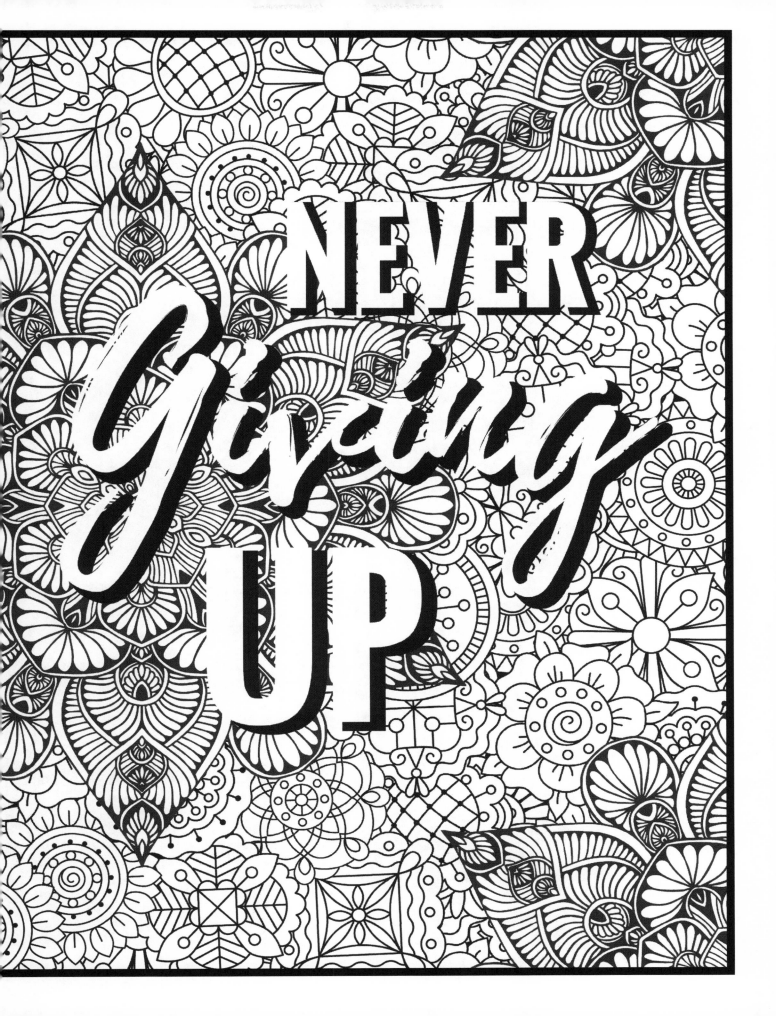

Date _____ M ☐ T ☐ W ☐ T ☐ F ☐ S ☐ S ☐

One goal for today

_____

Today's positive affirmation

_____

_____

My mood today   Did I stay sober today?

★ ★ ★ ★ ★   YES ☐   NO ☐

Was today's goal accomplished?

YES ☐   NO ☐

What I am grateful for today

_____

_____

_____

What I am proud of today

_____

_____

_____

My plans for tomorrow

_____

_____

Additional thoughts

Today's sketch

Date _____ M ☐ T ☐ W ☐ T ☐ F ☐ S ☐ S ☐

One goal for today

_____

Today's positive affirmation

_____

_____

My mood today   Did I stay sober today?

★ ★ ★ ★ ★   YES ☐   NO ☐

Was today's goal accomplished?

YES ☐   NO ☐

What I am grateful for today

_____

_____

_____

What I am proud of today

_____

_____

My plans for tomorrow

_____

Additional thoughts

Today's sketch

Date _____ M ☐ T ☐ W ☐ T ☐ F ☐ S ☐ S ☐

One goal for today

Today's positive affirmation

My mood today	Did I stay sober today?
★ ★ ★ ★ ★	YES ☐ NO ☐

Was today's goal accomplished?

YES ☐   NO ☐

What I am grateful for today

What I am proud of today

My plans for tomorrow

Additional thoughts

Today's sketch

Date _____ M ☐ T ☐ W ☐ T ☐ F ☐ S ☐ S ☐

One goal for today

_____

Today's positive affirmation

_____

_____

My mood today   Did I stay sober today?

★ ★ ★ ★ ★   YES ☐   NO ☐

Was today's goal accomplished?

YES ☐   NO ☐

What I am grateful for today

_____

_____

_____

What I am proud of today

_____

_____

_____

My plans for tomorrow

_____

_____

Additional thoughts

Today's sketch

Date _____ M ☐ T ☐ W ☐ T ☐ F ☐ S ☐ S ☐

One goal for today

_____

Today's positive affirmation

_____

_____

My mood today   Did I stay sober today?

⭐ ⭐ ⭐ ⭐ ⭐   YES ☐   NO ☐

Was today's goal accomplished?

YES ☐   NO ☐

What I am grateful for today

_____

_____

_____

What I am proud of today

_____

_____

_____

My plans for tomorrow

_____

_____

Additional thoughts

_____

_____

_____

_____

_____

_____

_____

Today's sketch

Date _____ M ☐ T ☐ W ☐ T ☐ F ☐ S ☐ S ☐

One goal for today

_____

Today's positive affirmation

_____

_____

My mood today   Did I stay sober today?

★ ★ ★ ★ ★   YES ☐   NO ☐

Was today's goal accomplished?

YES ☐   NO ☐

What I am grateful for today

_____

_____

_____

What I am proud of today

_____

_____

My plans for tomorrow

_____

Additional thoughts

Today's sketch

Date _____ M ☐ T ☐ W ☐ T ☐ F ☐ S ☐ S ☐

One goal for today

....

Today's positive affirmation

....

....

My mood today   Did I stay sober today?

★ ★ ★ ★ ★   YES ☐   NO ☐

Was today's goal accomplished?

YES ☐   NO ☐

What I am grateful for today

....

....

....

What I am proud of today

....

....

....

My plans for tomorrow

....

....

Additional thoughts

Today's sketch

Date _____ M ☐ T ☐ W ☐ T ☐ F ☐ S ☐ S ☐

One goal for today

_____

Today's positive affirmation

_____

_____

My mood today   Did I stay sober today?
★ ★ ★ ★ ★   YES ☐   NO ☐

Was today's goal accomplished?
YES ☐   NO ☐

What I am grateful for today

_____

_____

_____

What I am proud of today

_____

_____

_____

My plans for tomorrow

_____

_____

Additional thoughts

Today's sketch

Date _____ M ☐ T ☐ W ☐ T ☐ F ☐ S ☐ S ☐

One goal for today

_____

Today's positive affirmation

_____

My mood today   Did I stay sober today?

★ ★ ★ ★ ★   YES ☐   NO ☐

Was today's goal accomplished?

YES ☐   NO ☐

What I am grateful for today

_____

_____

What I am proud of today

_____

_____

My plans for tomorrow

_____

Additional thoughts

Today's sketch

Date _____ M ☐ T ☐ W ☐ T ☐ F ☐ S ☐ S ☐

One goal for today

_____

Today's positive affirmation

_____

_____

My mood today   Did I stay sober today?

★ ★ ★ ★ ★   YES ☐   NO ☐

Was today's goal accomplished?

YES ☐   NO ☐

What I am grateful for today

_____

_____

_____

What I am proud of today

_____

_____

My plans for tomorrow

_____

Additional thoughts

Today's sketch

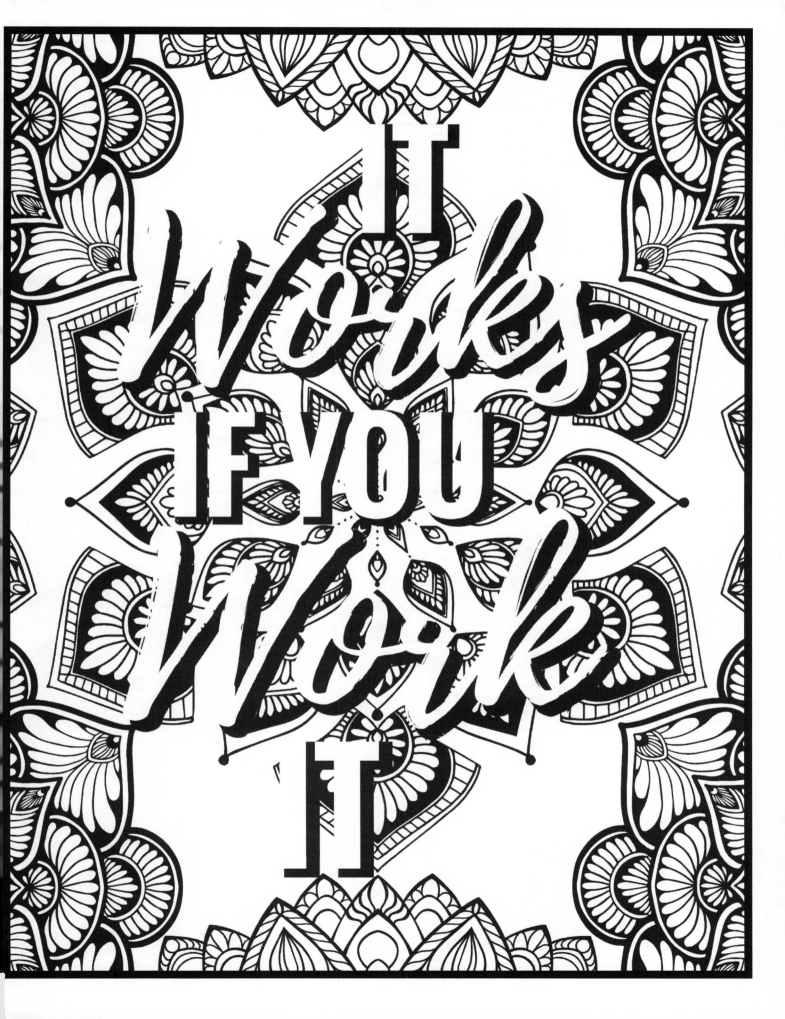

Date _____ M ☐ T ☐ W ☐ T ☐ F ☐ S ☐ S ☐

One goal for today

_____

Today's positive affirmation

_____

My mood today   Did I stay sober today?

★ ★ ★ ★ ★   YES ☐   NO ☐

Was today's goal accomplished?

YES ☐   NO ☐

What I am grateful for today

_____

_____

What I am proud of today

_____

_____

My plans for tomorrow

_____

_____

Additional thoughts

Today's sketch

Date _____ M ☐ T ☐ W ☐ T ☐ F ☐ S ☐ S ☐

One goal for today

_____

Today's positive affirmation

_____

_____

My mood today	Did I stay sober today?

★ ★ ★ ★ ★   YES ☐   NO ☐

Was today's goal accomplished?

YES ☐   NO ☐

What I am grateful for today

_____

_____

_____

What I am proud of today

_____

_____

My plans for tomorrow

_____

_____

Additional thoughts

Today's sketch

Date _____ M ☐ T ☐ W ☐ T ☐ F ☐ S ☐ S ☐

One goal for today

_____

Today's positive affirmation

_____

My mood today   Did I stay sober today?

★ ★ ★ ★ ★   YES ☐   NO ☐

Was today's goal accomplished?

YES ☐   NO ☐

What I am grateful for today

_____

_____

_____

What I am proud of today

_____

_____

My plans for tomorrow

_____

_____

Additional thoughts

Today's sketch

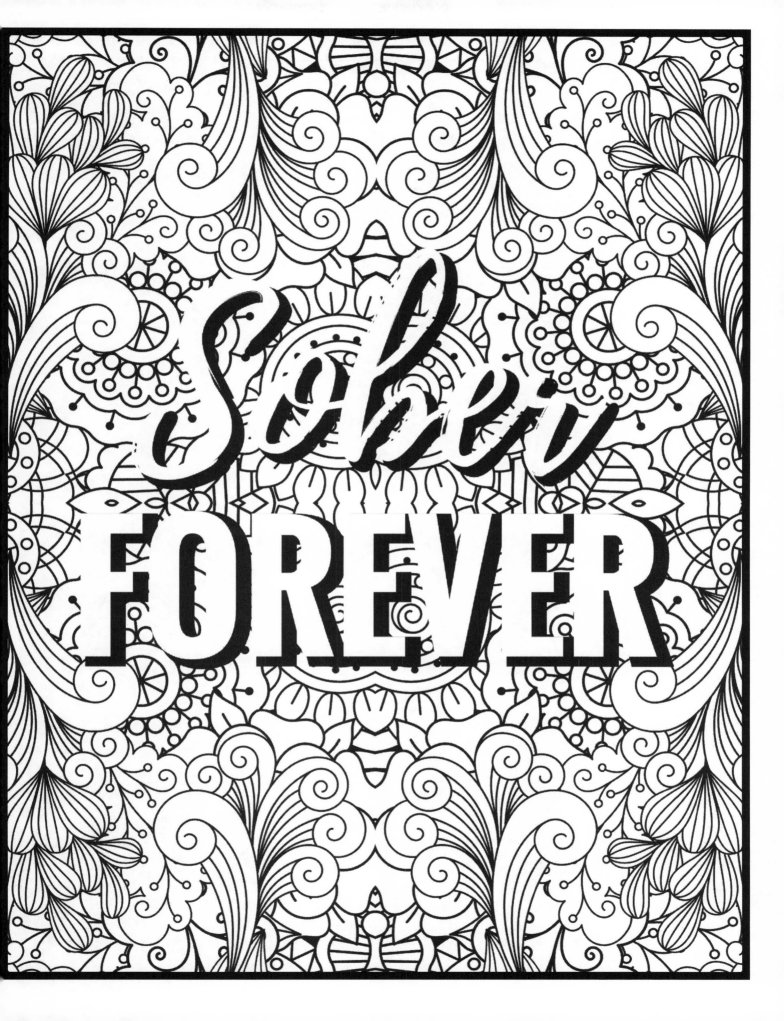

The 5 rules to create positive affirmations

- Always start with "I" or "My"

- Always use the present tense: say "I am" or "I feel" but not "I will" or "I should"

- Never use negations: say "I always succeed" and not "I never fail"

- Be precise and concise: don't say "I'm grateful" but "I'm grateful for having two awesome children"

- Always include a feeling

10 examples of positive affirmations

- My life is a joy filled with love, fun and friendship

- I'm a do-er : I take action and get things accomplished

- I finish every thing I start

- I'm responsible for everything happening in my life

- The universe provides for my every want and need

- I believe in my skills and abilities

- My body is a temple. I will keep my temple clean

- I make positive healthy choices

- I search for the good that comes even in bad situations

- I am so grateful for my life

Made in United States
Orlando, FL
09 January 2024

42323274R00055